Homecoming

Melinda Burns

Copyright © 2025 by Melinda Burns

All rights reserved. No part of this publication may be reproduced or transmitted in any form or by any means, electronic or mechanical, including photocopying, recording or any information storage and retrieval, without the written permission of the publisher. Names, characters, places and incidents are either the product of the author's imagination or used fictitiously, and any resemblance to actual persons living or dead, events or locales is entirely coincidental. All trademarks are properties of their respective owners.

Published by
BookLand Press Inc.
15 Allstate Parkway, Suite 600
Markham, Ontario L3R 5B4
www.booklandpress.com

Printed in Canada

Front cover design by Wendy Beaulieu

Library and Archives Canada Cataloguing in Publication

Title: Homecoming / Melinda Burns.
Names: Burns, Melinda, author.
Series: Modern Indigenous voices.
Description: Series statement: Modern Indigenous voices
Identifiers: Canadiana (print) 20250129485 | Canadiana (ebook) 20250129655 | ISBN 9781772312485 (softcover) | ISBN 9781772312492 (EPUB)
Subjects: LCGFT: Poetry.
Classification: LCC PS8603.U7432 H66 2025 | DDC C811/.6—dc23

We acknowledge the support of the Government of Canada through the Canada Book Fund. We acknowledge the support of the Canada Council for the Arts. We acknowledge funding support from the Ontario Arts Council and the Government of Ontario.

"Through love, all pain will turn to medicine."
~ *Rumi*

Introduction

I was not aware of the Medicine Wheel when I was growing up, though my mother was Mohawk, born and raised on the Six Nations reserve near Brantford, Ontario. She had been schooled in the belief that the ways of her people were inferior, their traditional practices belonging to the "Longhouse pagans," so she had no interest in passing them on to me. When I came upon the teachings of the Medicine Wheel as an adult, I felt a kinship and an opening to a way of understanding the world and our journey through life.

The Medicine Wheel is a symbol of balance and wholeness, pictured as a circle divided into four sections. The four quadrants represent many aspects of life such as the four directions — East, South, West, and North; the four times of day — dawn, mid-day, afternoon, evening; the four aspects of humans — spiritual, physical, mental, and emotional; and the four seasons — spring, summer, autumn, and winter. Each quadrant has a corresponding animal — Eagle, Mouse/Coyote, Bear, and White Buffalo, and a colour — yellow, red, black, and white. The order may differ slightly with different traditions.

When it came time to organize these poems, they seemed to naturally fall into four sections relating to the powers of the four directions of the Medicine Wheel.

The East signifies new beginnings, birth, dawn, springtime, the many ways we start out or start again—the early days of life or of a relationship, the birth of a child, a sense of newness or discovery with the accompanying hopes and fears.

The South is the place of innocence and joy, summer time, celebration, the awakening of the senses to nature, to relationship.

The West represents introspection, the season of autumn, going within to understand more, spiritual trust and transformation, loss, maturing into middle age.

The North is the place of the Elder, the ancestors, of wisdom gathered, winter time, gratitude for the lessons of life.

And the Centre is the place of the Creator and of the Great Mystery at the heart of everything.

We travel through and around the Medicine Wheel in a lifetime with a weaving of the teachings brought forth from each direction. These poems reflect my path so far. I offer them with abundant thanks to my ancestors, my family and friends and my daughter, who all guide and sustain me in this ongoing homecoming.

~ Guelph, Ontario, 2024

Table of Contents

East: Beginnings

Gesture | 13
Pancake | 14
Kitchen Story | 15
My Mother's Kitchen | 16
Cold | 17
How to Build a Time Machine | 18
The Closed Bedroom Door | 19
Scenes from a Marriage I | 20
Shopping | 21
The Unmaking | 22
Saved | 23
Swaddling | 24
Interrupted Poem | 25
Finches | 26

South: Innocence

Hillside Festival | 29
Home Street Gallery | 30
The Lovers | 31
Piano Lesson | 32

Adolescence in Suburbia | 33
Heart in the Sky | 34
Scrabble | 35
Baby Steps | 36
Heat | 37
Scenes from a Marriage II | 38
Sugar | 39
Night Song | 40
Heat Wave | 41
Offering | 42
Speed Date and Dance | 43
On Knocking the Head Off the Buddha Statue | 44

West: Going Within

Therapy During COVID | 47
The Feast | 48
Scenes from a Marriage III | 49
Lakers on a Good Night | 50
Clearings | 51
Rain | 53
Valentine | 55
Giants | 56
Mother of Mine | 57
Matrilineal Forbears | 58
Walls | 59
Connection | 60
Sanctuary | 61
Life Force | 62
Love Story | 63
Languaging | 64

North: Elder/Wisdom

Writing Retreat | 67
Positioning | 68
Vulnerable | 69
Going Home | 70
Bringing the News | 72
After You Died | 73
The Moment I Was Born a Girl | 74
Hindsight | 75
My Native Mother Mourns the Queen | 76
Sage | 77
Dear Mother | 78
Scenes from a Marriage IV | 79
Heart | 80
More | 81
Living Alone | 82
The Path | 83
Homecoming | 84
Ode to Winter | 86
Orange Shirt Day | 87

Centre: The Great Mystery

How to Write a Poem | 91
Medicine | 92
Prayer | 93

EAST
Beginnings

Gesture

It would be night, travelling somewhere
by car, my father driving,
my mother in her black Hudson's seal coat
that I would lean into if I were
in the front between them

They think I'm asleep on the back seat
My mother draws a cigarette from his pack of Sweet Caps,
puts it to her lips, though she doesn't smoke,
lights it from the glowing end
of the push-in dashboard lighter

then leans toward him, I see her,
to place it between his lips,
a gesture of such intimacy that
I don't make a sound but settle
down in my seat and fall asleep

Pancake

My father didn't cook
Two older sisters and a mother
and then his wife, my mother
took care of all his food needs.
"A good eater," my mother
called him, meaning not picky,
ate everything, appreciated it.

But some weekend mornings
he made pancakes for us,
large ones, big as the plate,
one each for my brother and me,
slathered in butter and maple syrup,
or more likely, margarine
and maple-flavoured syrup,
but it was the size, big as the plate,
and that he made them,
that made them wonderful.

Kitchen Story

My mother says she has something to tell me,
turns to me from the stove where potatoes
boil and bump in the pot

I stand still to hear, a bundle of forks
in my hand for the table

You are half Indian she says

and a thrill runs through me
like finding out I'm part dragonfly

*But when you go to school, if anyone asks,
say you're of English descent*

like my father, not like her
I nod, another thing to know

like keep your dress down
so your underpants don't show,
don't talk about vomit at the supper table,

don't say you're Indian.

I place the forks carefully,
one on the left side of each plate,
as I've been taught.

My Mother's Kitchen

My mother's kitchen
was small and dark
though there was a window
over the kitchen table
she faced away from
standing at the stove

The walls were green
and there was linoleum
that didn't show anything
and the smell of meat
and potatoes
and something like
discontent, simmering

Who will come in and
untie the apron from
my mother's waist
spin her around toward the light
sit at the table with her
while she writes the note
that says she's leaving
for a while

When the family comes home
we smell the meat
and potatoes
and some new scent
we've never smelled
before

Cold

The coldest time was waiting for the bus in winter,
standing at the stop, stepping foot to foot,
craning to see if it's coming

My mother and I, on the way to my piano lesson,
so important to her that I learn to play.
Big black upright bought for my brother
and when he lost interest
I became the one

And so we would stand, in the late afternoon
winter dark, waiting,
music books in a folder
clutched under my arm

Snow falling all around us,
my mother's dreams
piling up on me

How to Build a Time Machine

You gather cardboard
(leftover refrigerator cartons are best)
rubber bands, masking tape and
paint, and an old clock
with hands you can move

You build it in the backyard
or next to the furnace in the basement
and you only tell people who
believe in you
(never your brother)

When it's finished, you get in
crouch down,
push the painted button
wind the clock hands back
                 or ahead…

step out
    to the time
        before you had to leave kindergarten
      or the time
          after you cared what people thought

The Closed Bedroom Door

On one side
the daughter
at her desk, writing.
Writing in her journal
spilling out in code
not even she can decipher
news of boys and
school assignments
standing in for what
she really wants,
the wings to fly
to where her life
begins

On the other side
the mother
on the couch reading.
Reading of failed movie stars'
failed lives
thinking of dinner
and what needs
doing next
always something
listening to the clock tick
listening for the door to open
for the daughter
                to come through

Scenes from a Marriage

I

They stand on a mountain top, surrounded by friends
she in a loose white cotton dress,
he in an embroidered shirt
their faces shining in the dappled sun.
Their vows are homemade,
her bouquet gathered from a friend's garden
After the ceremony each guest floats a flower
down the mountain stream
with wishes for the couples' future.

Shopping
(for Ksenia)

You won't remember it—the day you took me shopping
to the high-end stores I'd never enter,
for my birthday, a month or so after the miscarriage

"Try this one," you said, pulling expensive items
from the racks. "Let me buy them for you."
The fitted denim shirt, the long, yoked skirt.

"So Santa Fe," the hostess at the restaurant
said that evening

You, the mother friend, indulging me,
wanting me to be happy, consoled, lifted
and I, the cherished child, bereft
but feeling oh, so loved

The Unmaking

My mother always spoke of birth
with revulsion

If I asked, as a child,
"What was it like?"

"Don't remind me,"
my mother would say

shaking the shirt out on the
ironing board

Not to be spoken of, or just
"When I woke up, I had a baby."

I laboured in a well-appointed
birthing room, pink-patterned wallpaper

mid-wife and husband coaching
as I weathered contractions

barrelling down on me
like a twelve-wheeled semi

and in between,
the holy space of peace.

All my life I believed I could
not do this, could not bear this

and in those hours of labour
I was made, unmade and
made again into
a woman of my own

Saved

After that night
the endless, no sleep
fear-drenched, hopeless night,
when we'd taken her back to the hospital,

our newborn, pleaded with them
to relieve us of the terrible
burden of trying to keep her alive

so small, so new,
a broiling chicken
under the jaundice lights they'd loaned us
a tiny spark, days old
and we, like children ourselves
knowing nothing

        after that night
the day   the empty house
the useless light machine on the table.

Swaddling

The nurses taught me how to swaddle you
wrapping you in a blanket
like a burrito
tucking in the ends and each side
like a papoose
bundled in my arms

As you grew I carried you
in a sling next
to my heart
patting your puppy head
cradling
your small round bottom

You slept beside our bed
in a wicker laundry basket
the same one my mother used for me

Waking
I would turn to see you
waiting   eyes open
each of us attuned to inner clock
telling our time of need

Blanket to sling
basket to crib
room of your own
your world enlarges
you need me less

The nurses taught me how to swaddle you
No one has taught me
how to let you go

Interrupted Poem

How can anyone write a poem
when just at the crucial line
a voice calls from the bathtub
"Mama?"

and it all falls away.
all the momentum leading up
to that line
all the gathering and holding and
delicately balancing
the house of cards collapses
the line that was sinking
                    down
                        down
bobs to the surface

The poet is the mother
answering
the child is the poem
splashing.

Finches

The finches flock to the feeder
in alliterative profusion
and something new catches my eye

Is it? Could it be? Already?
I peer through binoculars
and there it is —

a hint of gold in the feathers, faint
but promising, forerunner to
the yellow of forsythia, daffodil

a turning from the drab
of his cold weather coat
to this reminder

this drop of sunshine
he becomes, sprinkle of spring
on this cold grey morning

SOUTH
Innocence

Hillside Festival

Dancing and clapping
shouting our joy
while musicians play
never wanting to stop

The man lifts his boy high
over his head and sets him
grinning, on his shoulders
both of them dancing

Poets stir the trees with
words rising, sun
spills through leaves

Newly tie-dyed shirts
spread out to dry,
an incandescent wash line

And everywhere music
on the wind, scent of
Aboriginal fire, burning
even through the monsoon rains

that swept us into tents
soaked and laughing
our shared disaster
And afterwards

rainbow arcing in the
clouds, the heavens
themselves tie-dyed,
everything shining

Home Street Gallery

Come with me, I say to my friend.
I want to show you something amazing.
We walk a few streets over to
what looks like a Little Library,
wooden cabinet on a pole,
glass door. But inside —

Tiny people looking at the walls
covered with tiny "paintings",
some just scribbles, some with haiku
written over flowers, some landscapes

and in the corner, in a plastic case,
marked "Supplies. Help yourself",
little squares of watercolour paper
"Take art. Leave art. Love art."

I took one, I added one
now on display

Look, I say to my friend,
Look at what's here
My friend takes a little square,
herself, to make a painting

All of us artists
All of us patrons

The Lovers

They sit close at their table,
her black hair, his dark beard,
peering at an open laptop

She leans in to kiss his cheek
arm over his shoulder
and we all pause at our tables —

look up as if we can feel it
radiating out, touching
memories or longing,
or just reminding us

that love exists
fleeting or enduring,
heartbreaking or sustaining

We bask in their glow.
as he smiles at her,
as she touches his arm

Piano Lesson

I remember the stairway from the street,
climbing the dark stairs with
music books under my arm
and poems in my head

She greets me, tall and white-haired,
Miss Blake, imposing as she
opens the door, welcoming a
small unpracticed girl

Before going to the piano,
she sits down at her old black typewriter,
listens to the poem I composed
on my way over,

something about autumn trees,
types it with her thick-veined hands
that will soon play Mozart for me

How did she know
my poems were my music?

Adolescence in Suburbia

This is a poem for you
in your unhatched egg
your suburban quarantine
suspended in amber
aimless time
waiting out your teenage sentence

Walking to the mall
to buy the frosted pink
lipstick you hope
might make the transformation,
glasses in your pocket
preferring to squint

nothing to see anyway
but look-alike houses and
rivers of cars

Poking at your hair
in the bathroom mirror
after tossing all night
on prickly brush rollers
and still

it goes up when you
want it to go down
and down
when you want it
to go up

Heart in the Sky

"A nation is not conquered until the hearts of its women are on the ground."
~ Cherokee proverb

I come to my daughter's classroom
to speak of being Native,
pass around the smudge pot
from my mother's reserve,
the sage and sweetgrass I burn
to carry prayers to heaven

> *In school we painted murals of*
> *teepees and dark-skinned people*
> *on long brown butcher paper,*
> *made longhouses from*
> *Popsicle sticks*
> *I never said I was Indian*

I hold up the drum I made
the dancing turtle I painted
on its deerskin face
My daughter's classmates
file past, wide-eyed

bang the drum with the beater
trace the turtle with wondering fingers
"Cool," they say

Scrabble

"Let's have a game," my mother says
and I grudgingly fold out the long
spindly legs of the card table, bring out
the bag that holds the little tiles

We sit across, each behind our
ledge of letters, puzzling out
possibilities, bemoaning the
lack of vowels

"I have nothing," she says,
"nothing at all" before adding a Z
and an E before my BRA,
the ten-point Z on a triple-letter square

raking in the 37 points
like a lucky blackjack player
"Good word," I say as I add my S
ahead of her MILE and smile

We play to win, mother/daughter
rivalry played out on this
board, not considering
the other's feelings

Whatever works and each
for herself. "You rascal, you
stole my spot," she says
without rancor, and then pores
over her shelf of letters, plotting
her next move

Baby Steps

Saul the physiotherapist
is helping my father to walk

"Put your hands here, Tom,"
he says. "Push yourself up."

My father, thinner and frailer
than I've ever seen him, a stick man

his head bowed, mouth open
pushes on the wheelchair arms

Saul hauls him up by the waistband
I imagine no weight at all

Little steps with the walker
Saul with a tight grip on
the back of his pants

I run ahead, walk backwards before him
"Lift your head, Tom," Saul says. "Do you
see your daughter?"

He looks up   I go back
in time   my baby steps
towards him

And did he say then, as I do now,
"That's it. That's the way.
Good for you!"

Heat

The moment I go back to—
the organic farm, the rows of plants,
a hillside in the California sun

Had we broken up by then, one of the times?
a chance reunion, a kiss,
then falling to the dirt, kissing more

Moving to your room in the loft
to make love but that isn't
what I remember

not the taking off of clothes
not the bed, the light through the window
not the aftermath when we parted again

but the warm earth and the plants greening
and our bodies, hungering for each other
in the California sun

Scenes from a Marriage

II

They sleep curled together
she behind him, her hand on his heart
feeling the life in him beat
in her fingertips,
sure they are truly at the heart
of one another
and always will be

Sugar

After her fourth session with the new therapist,
she rode her bike down to Sugar Beach
by the lake, and watched
a crane on a freighter scoop up
sugar from the refinery, open
over the hold on the ship,
white grains raining down

Then she rode to Kensington market
for groceries, stocking up on all
the things she needed, this girl who would
call me in tears, overwhelmed
with adult life, unable to take
the dishes from her room to the kitchen
one floor below let alone cook herself a meal.

Such is the power of someone paid
to listen, who creates metaphors for
what she says, holding them out
like beacons to light her way home.
She sounds so light on the phone
as she tells me they're talking of
"hard stuff but it's good"

and then she says "I love you, Mom. I
seriously love you. Thanks for being such a
good mom, for having my friends over and
making cookies and arranging birthday
parties, and holding me when I cried…"

on and on, things from years ago, things I
hardly remember, a pause and then
another list, pouring sugar down
all over me

Night Song

My daughter is recording birds' night song
outside her third floor room in Toronto
trying to figure out what kind of birds they are

She sends the recording to me
thinking I might know —

I don't, but I listen

to their heartfelt notes pouring
out in the darkness
while we are all confined

in a pandemic night
I open my windows
Drink it in

Heat Wave

The stone Buddha presides
over the heat-ravaged garden,
eyes cast down, hands in lap,
like a grieving god

dried stalks of plants, hard-packed earth,
melting glaciers and wind-whipped wildfires
the stone fish gasps for breath

But further along —
the russet-coloured Heuchera,
almost gone,

sends up a sudden spray of
tiny coral bells —
a red flare signaling

Still alive! Still alive!

Offering

"Do you want to hear a poem?" I ask
the older woman standing in front of me
in the thrift store line-up

We've just bonded over the vintage
Ian and Sylvia record
that she's buying for her son
"He's crazy for vinyl," she says.

So I read her a short Wendell Berry poem
from the back cover of the collection
I found for a dollar on the shelf,

"This Day," about heat-curled leaves
and thirsty air, and it finishes,
after seven short lines, with
If tonight the world ends /
we'll have had this day

"Isn't that lovely," she says,
and then she moves forward
to pay for her record.

Speed Date and Dance

I carried the flyer around with me
for weeks, tried to talk a friend
into going, so we could laugh
about it, the 50 – 65 age group,
scheduled earlier in the evening
than the other groups.

I love to dance, but as the weeks passed
it sounded too excruciating — the hopefulness
of dressing up, the reliving of high school,
and in the end, I couldn't
imagine any man I'd like to meet
would be willing to go through
such an event.

Instead I invited my neighbour
for dinner and we laughed ourselves silly
over quiche and wine and called it
a night.

                And yet, this morning,
I keep noticing men, grey-haired, lean,
my age, reading the paper, tapping on laptops
at this café and I want to slide into a chair
opposite, start a conversation, see
if we can dance.

On Knocking the Head Off the Buddha Statue

An urge to re-position the hostas around
the plaster Buddha in the rock garden—
Stepping around and over him,
traversing the little hill,

the uncertain rocky places,
my foot catches—
       he tumbles forward,
              his head hits the stone—

I thought it smashed and gone
but the break is clean,
head separated from body
as is my own some days

I carry the severed parts,
to the table,
squeeze the last bit
of Krazy glue along the edges

Then, clamping them together,
my fingertips rough with glue residue,
I place my hand on his head,
close my eyes and press down,
pray for wholeness

WEST
Going Within

Therapy During COVID

We talk by phone while they walk,
quieting when others pass by
or from their cars parked on
side streets or in their driveway

or from their bedroom, whispering in case
a parent or roommate is near
We talk while their children
text them, needing attention

The trickling sound of water
From my garden fountain
accompanies, and my cat
might wander in

Birds frequent the feeders
and the cedars sway in the wind
Rain patters on the skylight

And all the while, their voices
speak of work worries,
relationship tangles,
troubled children

All the while
a virus keeps us distant
calling out to one another
Can you hear me?

The Feast

The feast you are offering
is a gritty fare:
salty broth of effort
bitter greens of grief
tough and fibrous sinews
of discontent
simmering for years

We go to restaurants
order lavishly as if we could
feed our hungry hearts
with dishes from a menu

But all they have is food
and in me the milk
of human kindness
is curdling over time

I'm living on memories
fasting on doubt
growing thinner than a
spoon

Scenes from a Marriage

III

They stand in the kitchen late into the night
he is leaning on the counter, she is by the window
He's found an apartment to move to. They haven't
told their child. The ceiling light
hits the white ceramic tile floor, the white counter,
the white walls, too bright

Lakers on a Good Night

I remember watching the games
on TV in California,
the time we rented a car and
drove down to L.A. just to see
them play

"Like the Lakers on a good night," you
called us in the early days, the way
we moved with liquid grace, effortless
weaving, smooth passes, high-five celebration
at having found each other

Adding a baby and moving the team
to Canada, our passing faltered,
we grew clumsy, each of us
driving for the basket,
opposing teams, pulling apart

And then divorce,
       the ultimate trade,
the child bouncing back and forth
between us

We're in different leagues now
don't even meet for games, neither of
us in the championship finals

The late great Lakers, devoid of
Magic, memories of our glory days,
when we owned the court.

Clearings
(*Santa Barbara Tea Fire, 11/13/08*)

My friend stands in the
panoramic mountain view
of her once house, now
nothing but a concrete foundation
and a stone fireplace
charred palm trees all around
like battle-scarred sentinels

She walks me through where the
kitchen was, the hallways, the
children's bedrooms, full of memories
But it is when she speaks of the trees
they had to take down—jacaranda,
pepper, acacia—that she begins to
cry. "It broke my heart," she says

The house will be rebuilt, smaller
She and her husband
drive up from their rental house to
water the ground every day

Red hollyhocks bloom
where red flames licked
The green is coming back

I think of my marriage,
the separation, like
a burning to the ground of
a house thought solid

Or maybe the divorce is like
the removal of the foundation,
only memory left of rooms and years

And the trees taken out are like the
dreams of growing old together —
irreplaceable, not enough time to
grow them with someone else

The detours our lives take,
the strange clearings
the way the green comes back

Rain

The rain pours down on Yonge Street
outside the Starbucks where I wait
with chai tea while my daughter sees
a new therapist.

We laughed on the way, under our two
umbrellas as mine dripped on her neck,
that now she'd have material to talk
to the therapist about.

She has plenty of material to talk
to a therapist about — two "complicated"
parents, as she calls us, estranged
after a deadly divorce,

a sensitive nature that makes her the
wonder she is and the despairing
being she becomes at times.   I want

this fifty-ish woman with the gray-blonde
hair and the flowing clothes
to hear her like she's never been heard,

through her tears that pour
like rain, to the heart of her troubles
that she believes are insoluble.   I want

her to offer no platitudes, no easy
answers, no answers at all that
would only fall short.   I want

her to be a presence for this girl and
her complicated feelings, a place
to pour them out to someone

who never birthed her, never
nursed her, never held her
and vowed to keep her safe

from all this rain.

Valentine

You call me in the midst
of a panic attack
engulfed in fear like flames,
the burning reasons
in your mind not as crucial
as the visceral threat
that wracks your body
as you reach for some ground,
my voice, to cling to
hold you

Later in the day, I take
the Valentine's package
I'm sending to you to
the post office, bubble-wrapped
heart-shaped glass
to hang in your window
as I would send you my heart
to beat alongside yours
until it calmed and
you could breathe again

Giants

My mother and my father
were giants once
the makers of life
in charge of the world

Now they are little
old people who don't hear,
fear falling, forget
where they're going

They cling to me
to keep life in order,
hold them up
as if I know what to do

Don't they know?
As long as they are here
I am a child

Mother of Mine

Mother of mine
Were you not born
Mohawk?
Is it not in your blood,
your mother and father and how far back?

Whose tales did you hear?
What stories of the old days,
the old ways?
"Longhouse pagans" you call them now,
with a sweeping phrase
overturning the past and
your rich heritage

I know about the drunkenness
the poverty
the indignity
I know I don't know the half of it
traded for a home in the suburbs,
pictures of the Queen,
neighbours you didn't care for
and stayed aloof from,
home permanents and
Easter outfits and a life of scrutiny
to see if you're White enough

Am I wrong?
Did you choose knowingly
with no regrets?
Is it only I,
your daughter,
who longs for what you left behind?

Matrilineal Forbears

The poet, Mary Tallmountain, says
she speaks every morning
to her matrilineal forbears—
her grandmother, two aunts, her mother
We talk about how my spirit is getting on
I lay before them my problems

I call on my ancestors in the morning
but they are abstract to me,
distant spirits I hardly know
My grandmother, a photograph
framed on my piano

I know nothing of my mother's
spirit, her wisdom
I never asked and now,
in her deaf old age,
I would have to shout

Mother, can you help me?!
I want to be whole!

Walls

The phone pings: my daughter
sending me a photo of her day —
dawn light edging the downtown buildings

as she prepares to go to work.
I send back a picture of my beginning —
notebook, pen, and glasses on my desk

Imagine if my mother
could have sent me a photo —

freshly-washed clothes
just rung out on the line,

and I sent back a picture
of the garden — light-gilded hostas,
burgeoning begonias

If we could have shared our worlds
instead of maintaining the walls
we both erected early on

against the terrible threat
of each other

Connection

All night I lay awake
as if it were me starting a new job today
not my daughter, imagining her
anxious about it, not able to sleep
and fretting more

How long does this go on,
this carrying the child who is
no longer a child, as if
nine months in the womb
welds us, heart and body,
for all our days

       This morning
the sun revives me from my
sleepless night, and she
sends me pictures of her
on the way to work, outfit
perfect, new shoes, new bag,
Like the first day of school!

And I remember bicycling after
the yellow school bus that took her away
to kindergarten, watching
from the edge of the schoolyard
until she flowed in with the others

And now, as then, she's fine
as she steps into the excitement
of a new place, a new phase,
that I feel along with her,
heart to heart, continuing

Sanctuary

I look up to hear
my friend's soft snoring
as she sleeps on the couch across from me,
curled on her side,
under the turquoise afghan.
How sweet a sound while
I read on my own couch.
A friend whose mother
died last week, who came
for tea and talk
and now, taking her rest,
falls asleep
finding sanctuary on my couch
as the afternoon sun
dims to evening.

Life Force

My neighbor calls me an Angel of Mercy
for drowning the injured mouse I found on my lawn
but she didn't see it struggle for life
throw out its little legs, churning the water

I thought it would just die,
let me put it out of its misery,
help it on its way
I didn't know how hard a creature

tries to stay alive, how adamant
they are, even injured
even for painful, lingering life

I remember my mother's
ragged breaths, persisting
all the way to the end

Love Story

The glass polar bear looks
longingly at the stone Buddha,
each immobile on the desk

The Buddha smiles, would
reach a hand to pat the polar head

compassion for its vanishing
ice home. The bear leans
in to the Buddha

Tell me how to be, O Wise One,
how to bear my sorrow.
No pun intended, she adds

The Buddha smiles.
Dear One, he says, bearing
is all – the sorrow, the fear

Your home is in this very place
Let us bear together.

Languaging

The Mohawk language is based on verbs
not nouns, not the names of static things—
table, river, friend—but the way of
tabling, rivering, friending that they or we do,
everything in motion, interacting,
changing form.

> My grandfather taught me a few words
> of Mohawk when I was small,
> a call and response, a greeting, maybe
> I wrote love letters to him on his old black
> typewriter with its round, metal-rimmed keys,
> banging out lines of letters before I knew
> how to read, the verb of my love
> flowing all along the lines.

The language is becoming lost,
fewer and fewer people able to speak it
though there are schools now
teaching people to use it again
in their everyday lives, while they're
childing, grandfathering,
living in all the moving parts.

NORTH
Elder / Wisdom

Writing Retreat

In the evening they walked
through blizzards of black flies
Five women, side by side,
on the empty gravel road,
semi-protected by bug spray,
talking of writing, talking of living
in the long never-ending day

Positioning

I like to position things
for ease, for convenience,

for aesthetics—the pitcher of red and yellow tulips
on the table nearby

The lamp for more light to read by,
a big chair turned toward the window for a better view

The placement of things
matters to me, and yet,

without my help,
every rock in this river is exactly right

Vulnerable

The doctor tells me he's found
something in my mother's stomach,
the size of a baseball, he says,
and what do I want him to do?
She's 94, he says,
as if I don't know

The next day I drive her to a funeral,
her brother's wife, and
as we sit side by side
for the two-hour drive
I can't tell her

She is so deaf and
this is not a conversation for shouting,
not a conversation for before
or after funerals

Just this week we arranged
for the retirement home apartment
that finally came available.
She and my father hugged the woman
who showed it to them
like relieved children.

Going Home

My father sits in his wheelchair
at the hospital where he's been
for four months

They tell him today he's going home
He lifts his head to hear the news
let it in down the long darkening halls
of his consciousness

bringing him back from his travels
on the troop train in World War Two
where he thinks he's been

Does he remember home, the apartment
in assisted living where he sat
on the balcony in September sun

or will he expect his boyhood house
on Coleridge Avenue, or our first house
on Durant, or maybe the house they left
last year on Galbraith?

And will they dress him in the shirt and pants
he made sure were there so many times
ready for going home?

Will they put his feet in real shoes
or still his plaid slippers?
And when they take him down

to the waiting ambulance
will he look back?
Or only lift his head

to sniff the winter air
before they take him on
to the next place

Bringing the News

Her face lights up to see me
I sit beside her on the couch
hold her arthritis-bent hand, tell her
Dad's passed away

My father, her husband of sixty years,
the hospital called me last night
I drove this morning to tell her

"Oh," she says, tears
leaking down her cheeks
"Oh," and holds my hand
"We'll just have to be strong."

She hugs me close,
smaller than my own child,
takes off her glasses
wipes her eyes
gets up to put the kettle on
for tea

After You Died

I keep the few things
I found in your pockets, Dad

Two dimes, a nickel,
and three pennies
(*coppers* you would say)

A pack of matches
two left inside

I picture your hands
touching these things —

cupping the matches
for the cigarettes
you weren't supposed to smoke

jingling the change
in your pockets
as you came up the walk

whistling
a tune that was
all your own

The Moment I Was Born a Girl

I thought her life was in my hands
and I held it, packed it with me

carefully, through every move
                 Across the country and back

I thought my life was hers to use
I shaped myself to her necessities

whatever else I would become
a daughter was who I was

                After the funeral
something changed —

           the light
the space around my body

I could not help her now
I could not work the miracle

I left her then, in other hands
       and moved
             like a woman
                   freed from concrete

Hindsight

Many days I think of ways
I could have made my mother's life better
Twenty years now since she died

I could have brought her tea
in a cup with a lid to keep it hot
the way she liked it, could have

made her soup and cinnamon buns,
and brought her chocolate-covered
cherries every time I came.

Could have read to her and
asked about her years growing up
and what she was proud of,

and what she regretted. I could have
listened to her complaints about
growing old with more sympathy

now that I understand them more.
But I was steeped in a daughter's
obligation to make up for

her life's disappointments and
it seemed like all I could do
was resist

My Native Mother Mourns the Queen

You would have liked the Mounties,
their red coats shining, their horses proud
There would have been a tear
as the casket passed by, draped
in gold with wreaths of flowers,
pulled on the gun carriage
by scores of uniformed young men

You would have remembered
the young queen, the one whose picture
hung on our dining room wall,
her coronation, the births
of each of her children,
the Christmas message
we tuned into every year

You would have mourned her,
the same age you were
when she died,
the Great White English mother
who ruled over the land
that once belonged to your people

Sage

Pouring rain on a Saturday morning and
I light the lavender-sage candle
bought last week from the Ojibway woman
in the Anglican church parking lot

And from the candle, I light
a grey curl of sage from the bundle
I ordered on-line that arrived in a
cardboard box this week

I imagine my ancestors smiling
at the traditions continuing,
maybe even my mother, for all her
disdain for "Longhouse pagan" ways

Maybe she's an Elder now
in the way she was always meant to be,
wise in the ways of her people,
still killing it at scrabble in heaven

Dear Mother

In writing about you
I set you down

Remove you from my shoulders,
from carrying you
for so long

I am not your saviour, your redeemer
Not your condemner, your indictor

I will not turn on you,
Not snarl and bite
To rip my way free

You are not me
I am not you

I set you down
Softly, gently,
with love at last

I set you down
I set you down

Scenes from a Marriage

IV

They sit in the high balcony of Convocation Hall
Far below in a sea of black robes sits
their child, directly across so they can wave
Ten years since they've sat down together
outside a lawyer's office. They train their focus
on the girl below, shine down
on her like a spotlight. Their daughter says after,
"Seeing you up there, laughing and talking,
was like heaven."

Heart

Broken love affairs, broken
marriage, broken friendships
press on the heart, crazed
like a dropped blue vase, cracked
like a frost-heaved flowerpot
splintered like a slippery glass
dropped from dishwater

All these containers
and yet, the heart
goes on, self-repairing
in ways unknown
to continue its holy work
of holding what comes,
what goes

More

In the evening, I pause the TV,
gather up my wine glass,
my square-shaped bowl, my water glass,
and walk them to the kitchen

The same movement each time,
wine glass and water glass pinched together
in one hand, bowl and napkin in the other,
a winding down of the day

I know a woman whose life changed
in a matter of months — Alzheimer diagnosis,
lost her license (she loved to drive), house sold,
moved to a retirement home in another town

No stove, no cooking, no grocery shopping,
no cleaning up after.
            I think of her as I
drive to the store, wash
the windows, bake cookies

and even in that nightly routine--
picking up the dishes,
over and over. That's what I want
more and more of

Living Alone

I know we're meant
to seek out others
of our kind and I did,
for too long I did

and learned to fold my wings
tight against my body,
synchronize my breath with theirs,
live small and not intrude
my ways on those who had
their own ways

so now
        I spread my wings that still
can fly, and breathe
in my own rhythm
this larger than expected life
that has been here all along

The Path

I'm building a path
from beautiful broken stones
laying them out
in a graceful curve
across the lawn
to the rock garden

I'm writing a new story
from beautiful broken moments
laying them down
across the page
to a place
I can call home

Homecoming

You are still the child
hanging out on the edges
of the baseball field yearning
to be asked to play

Still the child
who can run like the wind
and win the red ribbons
on the school field day

You are still the child
who wandered into the nurses'
graduation in your overalls
drawn by the sounds of celebration
and the pink iced cakes

Still the child
afraid your parents wouldn't
come back for you
when they left you to stay
for a week in the country

You are still the child who
pulled sunfish from the pond and
roamed the bush with
your cousins, looking for trilliums

Still the child
seeking your mother's love
in every which way,
trying to find the way in

This is why you matter
This is why I keep you near
so you know that you are loved,
that I won't leave you behind,
that you have a home with me

Ode to Winter

Writing an ode to winter
is not easy.
Pablo Neruda, at home in his
native Chile or exiled
in sunny Spain
never had to do it.

This morning the temperature is -25
with a wind chill warning.
A vicious nose-nipping
finger-tingling beast is on the loose
and this afternoon there is the promise
of freezing drizzle.

And yet,
there is the sun
shining like a blessing
in the ice blue sky,
on the new snow
fresh as a clean sheet

of paper where
the pencil marks of the long
bare trees and
the calligraphy of weed shadow
etch an ode to winter.

Orange Shirt Day

One by one I see them, paper signs affixed to wire,
stuck in the ground, then all at once, hundreds
lining the sidewalk and walkways of the high school

Orange hand prints,
and the names of residential schools
written on them, one with "Mohawk Institute"
my mother's school

Two girls in orange shirts hand out
orange flags to students coming off the bus
and I ask them for one

What would my mother make of this?
School children with "Every Child Matters"
on their shirts, the lines of handmade signs,

the orange flags?
Would she dismiss it, or
would it awaken something in her chest

as it did in mine, some swelling
of sorrow and pride
as I carry my orange flag downtown

CENTRE
The Great Mystery

How to Write a Poem

Forget everything you know about poetry
and remember this:
the poem is inside you

Never mind rhyme
or reason
Listen to your heartbeat
that's the rhythm
Listen for the words that
lift the veil to the other world
where you know what you know

The poem is there
waiting to be written
      by you
            only by you

Medicine

Take one poem every day
with or without water
take the words of poets
from all times and
lay them on your forehead
like wet rags

wrap them around your wounds
take ink of ocean colour and
write your soul
across the page
take pains
and joys

and weave them in a tapestry
to fly above the clouds
take words as seeds
take heart
dear heart take
heart

Prayer

For all beings who have ever been wounded, disappointed, who have suffered loss, been a fool, who have let people down, in short, everyone; and especially for artists, poets, writers, and lovers who are losing hope and belief in themselves and what could be...please hear this prayer

Give us eyes to see through obstacles
to dreams and possibilities and love
always offered if we know
where to look

Grant us ears to hear the whispers
of encouragement, the sighs
of forgiveness, the song
of everlasting hope

Give us the smell of success
on our own terms, the scent of
the right trail, the whiff of
what we most cherish

Grant us the taste of our own
goodness, the tartness of
empowered defiance, the savouring
of the fruits of our labour

Give us the touch of consolation,
the quickening
of desire, the caress
of freedom, the tickle of joy

May we be whole

May we be true

May we be love

May it be so

Acknowledgement

This book would not be here without the support and encouragement of many people: Miss Jesse Blake, my grade two piano teacher who typed up the poems I composed in my head on the way to my lessons; Perie Longo who let me be a Poet in the Schools in California; Sarah Selecky and Alison Pick, whose retreats were such balm for a writer's soul; my dear writer friends and companions, Kathleen Corrigan, Shira Musicant, K.D. Miller, Carol Morgan, Cathy Langlotz, Brenda Aherne, Barbara Kenney, Michael Kleiza, Bernie Burns, Enid Osborn, and James Crews. And all the participants from my on-line groups, classes, workshops, and retreats. And especially my ever-inspiring daughter, Emma Burns, cheering me on. A special thank you to the lovely ladies of the Red Brick Café in Guelph, Ontario, who brightened my Friday morning writing times with countless cups of chai tea over the years. And finally, to BookLand Press for giving this book a home. Thank you all.

I dedicate this book to Olive and Emma, my mother and my daughter.

www.ingramcontent.com/pod-product-compliance
Lightning Source LLC
Chambersburg PA
CBHW061751070526
44585CB00025B/2855